50 BEST FITNESS EXERCISES

A step-by-step guide to the best toning exercises

First published by Parragon in 2011

Parragon
Queen Street House
4 Queen Street
Bath BA1 1HE, UK
www.parragon.com

Text by Sara Rose, Faye Rowe, Lucy Wyndham-Read
  and John Edward Kennett
Designed by Stonecastle Graphics Limited
Compiled by Gillian Haslam
Cover pictures: *Top left* © Moment/Getty Images; *Bottom right*
© Moment/Getty Images; *All other images* © iStock.

ISBN: 978-1-4454-5385-9

Printed in Indonesia

Note:
As a precautionary measure, the publishers advise that anyone
intending to follow the exercise programmes outlined in this
book should first consult a qualified practitioner or therapist.

50 BEST
FITNESS
BEST
EXERCISES

A step-by-step guide to the best toning exercises

PaRragon

Bath · New York · Singapore · Hong Kong · Cologne · Delhi
Melbourne · Amsterdam · Johannesburg · Auckland · Shenzhen

CONTENTS

INTRODUCTION

The exercises in this book have been chosen to help you tone up all over, so you'll get balanced results. They are divided into different sections, standing, seated and floor exercises, and each exercise identifies which main area of the body is being worked. If you have a quick look through the book, you will find exercises devoted to targeting shoulders, arms, chest, stomach, thighs and buttocks. Each exercise is carefully explained with step-by-step instructions.

Many of the exercises also work your core muscles, such as those found deep within the torso. This helps to develop your core stability, which will help to prevent injury during exercise and correct your posture. Exercises that work your core stability require you to 'engage' your stomach muscles. You can do this by pulling in your tummy muscles towards your spine, being careful not to hold your breath. This should automatically cause you to stand or lie in a straight line and create the perfect position to carry out the exercise.

Before starting a new exercise plan you should seek advice from your GP, especially if you are pregnant or suffer from back pain, in order to rule out any reason why it wouldn't be suitable for you. Most of the exercises in this book are easy to do, but if you do find any exercises particularly difficult to carry out, then you should stop attempting to do them and seek advice from a qualified fitness expert before carrying on. The most important thing to remember is that it's better to work in your comfort zone, rather than push yourself too hard. It's also important to remember that even when an exercise requires you to fully extend your arms or legs, you keep your knees and elbows 'soft' (slightly bent) to help guard against possible injury.

It is very helpful to have a basic understanding of how your body works, and why it's important to have good posture, before you embark on an exercise routine. Being muscle-aware will help you to target the areas that you want to firm up and ensure you get the most from your workout.

HOW YOUR BODY MOVES

Your body's framework is the skeleton, made up of more than 200 bones that support your muscles and allow you to move. Muscles fixed to the ends of bones permit an enormous range of movement. However, joints and muscles that are not regularly exercised may become stiff and immobile, leading to pain and possible injury.

Muscles are made up of millions of tiny protein filaments that relax and contract to produce movement. Most muscles are attached to bones by tendons and are consciously controlled by your brain. Movement happens when muscles pull on tendons, which move the bones at the joints. Most movements require the coordinated use of several muscle groups.

POSTURE

The alignment of your muscles and joints is known as posture. If your 'posture' is consistently poor over a period of time, your muscles will be subjected to uneven stresses, leading to aching muscles and joints, tiredness, weakness and an increased risk of injury when exercising.

Good posture looks natural and relaxed, not slouched and hunched. When you are standing up, your neck should be in line with your spine, with your head balanced squarely on top, your shoulder blades set back and down and your spine long and curving naturally. Your hips when sitting should be straight. Good posture means sitting up straight with your feet flat on the floor and your lower back supported.

CHECK YOUR POSTURE

Stand sideways in front of a full-length mirror to assess your posture. Imagine there is a straight line drawn down the centre of your body. If your posture is spot-on, the line will pass through the centre of the ear lobe, the tip of the shoulder, halfway through the chest, slightly behind the hip and just outside the ankle bone.

It does take time to correct any postural deficiencies you may have but it is important to identify what your weaknesses are – for example, rounded shoulders – so that you can work on correcting these. The good news is that by training your core muscles you will be strengthening the core muscles that hold up your back and this will automatically improve your posture.

THE SPINE

The spine is an S-shaped, flexible curve that supports your skull, acts as a structural base to which your limbs, ribs and pelvis attach, and enables you to stand upright. It also provides movement for your trunk, allowing you to bend forwards, backwards and to the side, and twist. The spine has three natural curves: in at the back of the neck, outwards at the back of the ribcage and in again in the lower back (lumbar spine).

To protect your spine, you should aim to maintain its natural curve, particularly in the lumbar region. This is called putting your spine into neutral, and nearly every exercise in this book will require you to do this. It's essential that you can perform this manoeuvre correctly, so use the instructions on the following pages as a guide to this correct position.

Standing neutral

1. Stand tall against a wall with your buttocks and shoulders touching the wall. Keep your feet parallel and hip-width apart, with your weight evenly dispersed over both feet. Gently pull up through your legs, keeping your knees slightly bent, and pull your tailbone down towards the floor.

2. Place your hand between the wall and your lower back. The neutral position is slightly different for everyone, but it should feel comfortable and you should just be able to place the flat of your hand between your back and the wall. If you can only get your fingers through, your back is too flat and your pelvis is tilted too far forwards. If you can get your whole hand through, then your back is too arched and your pelvis too far back.

Sitting neutral

1. Sit up straight on a stool, chair or exercise ball with your weight evenly distributed over both buttocks. Keep your feet flat on the floor, and a distance of hip-width apart.

2. Look straight ahead and keep your spine and neck long. Pull your shoulder blades down towards the waist to stop your shoulders from hunching or slumping forwards.

3. The natural curves at your neck and your waist should be evident.

Lying down neutral

1. Lie down on your back with your knees bent and your feet flat on the floor, hip-width apart. Your spine will be flat against the floor, apart from the curve of the neck and the lower back.

2. Press your waist back onto the floor by tilting your pelvis back so that you lose the curve in your lower back. Now tilt your pelvis forwards so that your lower back over-arches. Then find the mid-point between these two extremes. You should be able to slip one hand under your waist and feel a slight gap between your back and the floor.

PROTECT YOUR SPINE WHILE EXERCISING

· Be conscious of your neck – it's fine to cradle the sides of your head with your hands, but avoid resting your head on your hands because you may pull on your neck.

· Keep your abdominal muscles pulled in – this will protect your lower spine.

· Exercise on a mat or other padded surface to prevent bruising.

· Always keep your knees slightly bent when performing leg exercises – straight-leg exercising makes your hip flexors pull directly on the spine, causing excessive strain on your lower back.

CORE MUSCLES

The core of your body is simply what's between the shoulders and hips – basically, the trunk and pelvis. The core is a crucial group of muscles, not only for sports, but for normal daily activities as well, because it comes into play just about every time you move.

The core acts to produce force (for example, during lifting), it stabilizes the body to permit other musculature to produce force (for example, during running) and it's also called upon to transfer energy (for example, during jumping). This is why it is so important that your core is fit and strong.

Your balance and coordination will be improved, and, most important of all, the stability that these muscles bring will help to keep your spine healthy and flexible.

What is core stability?

Core stability is the effective use of the core muscles to help stabilize the spine, allowing your limbs to move more freely. Good core stability means you can keep your midsection rigid without forces such as gravity affecting your movements. The positive effects of this include reducing the chance of injury, better posture, increased agility, greater flexibility and improved coordination and balance.

Core stability is necessary for everyday life, not just for sport. To pick up a child, for example, requires a core strength in order not only to lift the child but also to do it in a safe and efficient way that avoids you injuring yourself. Everyone can benefit from core strength, from atheletes looking for increased performance to those completely new to exercise.

Identifying the core muscles

The muscles you need to know about for improving your core stability are those that are arranged around your torso.

Abdominal muscles: The abdominal muscles support the spine, protect internal organs and enable you to sit, twist and bend.

Back muscles: There are two groups of back muscles that are important to core stability. The first group attaches between each of the vertebrae; the second along the whole length of the spine.

Pelvic floor muscles: These attach to the inside of the pelvis, forming a sling from the tailbone at the back to the pubic bone at the front. These muscles are vital for continence and help to maintain intra-abdominal pressure, which is key to stablization.

Trunk muscles: The trunk muscles fall into two categories. The inner trunk muscles are mainly responsible for stabilization and the outer trunk muscles are mainly responsible for movement. The inner and outer units work together to create spinal stability and enable movement.

GETTING STARTED

A good way to start is to spend a quiet afternoon looking through this book to help familiarize yourself with the various stretches and exercises. Each exercise is explained with step-by-step instructions, and is clearly illustrated so you will find them easy to follow. Once you've changed into your comfortable clothes, you should switch off the television or any telephones so you won't be distracted. Put on some soothing music (or lively, uplifting music, if that's more to your taste) to help get you in the mood.

WHAT YOU NEED

Wear several layers of comfortable clothing as you start to exercise to warm up your muscles, and gradually strip off some of these layers as you get warmer. Clothes should be loose, soft and made from a breathable fabric – shorts and a vest covered with jogging bottoms and a sweatshirt, for example, are ideal.

There is no need to invest in expensive gym equipment, but it is a good idea to use a non-slip padded exercise mat for safety and to prevent discomfort and bruising. Some of the exercises can be performed using a set of small dumb-bells or hand weights to increase the level of difficulty, but do not use weights if you are new to exercising or have back problems. You may choose to invest in a set of dumb-bells, which can be bought from most high-street sports shops. Choose a weight that's challenging, but not impossible to work with – the shop staff will be able to advise you.

Some of the exercises in this book use resistance bands and these are covered in more detail on pages 94–95. Another group of exercises use an exercise ball (also known as a Swiss ball) and you can find out more about these on pages 118–119.

YOUR WORKOUT SPACE

Designate an uncluttered space in your home that is warm and well ventilated and large enough for you to extend your arms and legs without knocking anything over. Ideally, there will be enough space to enable you to take at least five steps in all directions.

An exercise mat is a good idea to cushion your body when doing floor work. If possible, try to do your exercise routine in front of a full-length mirror so that you can keep an eye on what you are doing. This will help you to copy the poses shown in this book, and help you to understand if you are performing the exercise correctly.

MAKING TIME FOR EXERCISE

The key to a toned body, increased fitness and more energy is to exercise little but often. Aim to exercise three or four times a week. You'll feel the benefits even if you can only manage ten minutes at a time. As you become fitter and stronger, you'll find that you can easily increase the intensity and the length of time of your workout.

To start with, aim to do each exercise five times (also see the section on reps below), but remember that it is the quality of the movement that is important, not the quantity. Start gently and build up the number of exercises as you become fitter, until you can perform ten repetitions. Do not attempt to do too much, too soon.

This book has a variety of easy exercises that are designed to work all areas of the body, enabling you to create workout plans to target specific areas of the body and slot a workout into even your busiest day. Until you become familiar with your routine, you may find it easier to write down your programme of exercises; perhaps you might like to bookmark the relevant pages in this book so that you can move from one exercise to another without wasting time.

If you find that you're struggling to make time for exercise, try these top tips:

- Visualize how your body will look in, say, a month's time and how you will feel if you stick religiously to your exercise plan. It will help you to realize why doing the exercises every day is essential.
- Try setting your alarm half an hour earlier than you usually do to give you time to exercise first thing in the morning.
- Invest in some flattering sportswear – it will make you want to exercise.
- If morning is the best time for you to exercise, start the day with a cup of warm water and a slice of lemon – it will help to detox your system and focus your mind.
- If you prefer to exercise at the end of the day, you will probably feel too invigorated to go to sleep immediately after exercising, so schedule your session to include some relaxation time before bed.
- If you get bored easily, try adding different exercises – there are plenty in this book to choose from. As you get stronger and fitter, you will start to find some of them almost too easy, so try some of the more challenging ones.

WARM UP AND COOL DOWN

To help guard against injury and make your body as receptive to the exercises as possible, we've included a warm-up plan (*see* pages 20–29). Make sure you always start with the warm up (especially if you have just jumped out of bed) before moving on to your main exercise routine.

It is just as important to cool down after your exercise session as it is to warm up before you begin. As well as helping to prevent dizziness and a sudden drop in body temperature, cooling down and stretching gently realigns working muscles to their normal position in order to avoid potential tightness and stiffness – *see* the section on pages 150–159 for these stretches.

CONTROLLING YOUR MOVEMENTS

All exercises should be done slowly and in a meditative fashion. Concentrate on what you're doing, and think about how your body is responding to each exercise. If any action feels quick or jerky, or hurts, you're not doing it properly. Each movement should flow in a slow, gentle manner. This lets your muscles warm up and stretch naturally. It takes time to learn a more gentle approach to movement, but if you try to keep your body relaxed as you move, with practice your body will become used to performing the exercises naturally.

BREATHING

It may sound silly, but you must remember to breathe at all times. Correct breathing comes from the deepest area of the lungs, and benefits both your body and mind. But years of stress and poor lifestyle have left most of us with shallow, rapid breathing, whereby we use only the top third of our lungs.

Many people have a tendency to hold their breath as they hold certain poses, which isn't advisable. Make sure that you breathe deeply and slowly throughout the routine, because it will help to deliver oxygen to the muscles and make the exercises more effective. The correct way to breathe when exercising is to breathe in slowly through your nose (notice how your abdominal cavity rises as you do so), and breathe out slowly through your mouth. Make sure you continue to breathe in and out regularly throughout an exercise. And don't hold your breath – this will cause blood pressure to rise, which can be dangerous.

REPS AND SETS

Muscle-building exercises are done as a series of repetitions (reps). One repetition equals one exercise. A set is usually a group of ten repetitions but may consist of anything between five and 15 reps, depending on your level of fitness. The aim of repeating exercises is to work until your muscles feel tired, and over time this will strengthen them so that they can work even harder. It's important that you don't stop for more than a minute between exercises. Shorter recovery periods result in better muscles all round and improved muscle endurance. So keep going!

Above: *A repetition involves the complete sequence of movements in a single exercise. The four steps in this Roll-up using an exercise band (see page 112) are one rep.*

WARM UP

WAIST TWIST

Tempting though it is to save time by launching yourself straight into an exercise routine, if you don't warm up you are highly likely to injure yourself because cold muscles and joints are less flexible and more prone to strain.

It is important not to move your hips and knees during this exercise, but do feel free to move your arms like a hula dancer if it helps you get into the right mood!

1. Stand up straight with your spine in neutral, and your knees slightly bent (soft, rather than 'locked'). Keep your feet hip-width apart and your hands resting on your hips. Make sure your spine is in the neutral position.

2. Tighten your abdominal muscles by pulling your navel back towards your spine.

3. Keeping your hips and knees still, rotate your shoulders and head to the right, then return to the centre.

4. Now twist to the left, rotating your head and shoulders and keeping your hips and knees still.

5. Repeat this exercise a further five times on each side.

HIP CIRCLES

This exercise will mobilize your lower abdominal muscles. Try to make sure that only your pelvis is rocking rather than your torso.

1. Stand up straight with your knees slightly bent, feet hip-width apart, hands resting on your hips.

2. Tighten your abdominal muscles by gently pulling your navel towards your spine. This movement should feel light and subtle – do not suck in your waist or hold your breath.

3. Gently rotate your pelvis to the right, so that you are rotating in a full circle.

4. Repeat nine times to the right then circle ten times to the left.

3

MARCHING

This warming-up exercise will help to raise your body temperature and increase blood flow to the muscles. March on the spot for at least a minute, swinging your arms and gradually raising your knees higher as you go (but not so that you're goose-stepping). Make sure your breathing is deep and regular as you march. Once you feel warm, take the time to perform a few stretching exercises.

BENDS

With these exercises, bend only as far as is comfortable – you don't have to touch your toes. Remember, you'll be able to stretch further as you become fitter and more supple with exercise.

FORWARD BEND

1. Stand up straight with your feet hip-width apart and your knees slightly bent, rather than locked. Place your hands palm downwards on the front of your thighs.

2. Tighten your abdominal muscles by gently pulling in your navel towards your backbone.

3. Slowly slide your hands down your legs towards your toes. Try not to overarch your back.

4. Position yourself so you feel a stretch in the hamstrings at the back of your legs, but don't stretch so far that it hurts.

5. Hold for a count of three, then return to the centre.

6. Repeat four more times. Keep your breathing steady throughout.

CAUTION
Never stretch to the point of pain.

4

3

FLATTER STOMACH IN A FLASH

A very simple way of making your stomach look flatter is simply to make sure your posture is correct. Good posture happens when your spine is in natural alignment, rather than hunched or slouched. For an instant, more streamlined appearance, stand with your feet hip-width apart. Gently pull up through your legs, keeping your knees slightly bent. Lengthen your spine, pull in your stomach muscles and stand tall. Keep your shoulders down and relaxed so that your neck is as long as possible, and as if by magic, your stomach will look flatter!

SIDE BENDS

Do not do this exercise quickly with your arms above your head because this will make it hard to control the movement.

1. Stand up straight with your feet hip-width apart and your knees slightly bent, with your arms by your sides.

2. Tighten your abdominal muscles by gently pulling your navel towards your spine.

3. Keeping your back straight and without leaning forwards, slowly bend to one side from the waist so that your hand slides down the side of your leg. Straighten up again.

4. Repeat on the other side. Repeat four more times on each side.

KNEE BENDS

This exercise loosens the hip flexor muscles and helps warm up all the leg muscles. Don't lock your knees as you do this, and bend only as far as is comfortable.

1. Stand with one hand resting on a support, such as a high-backed chair or a table, with your feet hip-width apart and slightly turned out. Tighten your abdominal muscles.

2. Slowly bend your knees and lower your hips, then straighten up again. Use your buttock and leg muscles to lower and straighten.

3. Repeat nine times.

2

LEG SWINGS

This exercise warms up the hip joints. Don't swing your legs too high (about 45 degrees is high enough), and keep the movements controlled and flowing.

1. Stand with one hand resting on a support, such as a high-backed chair or a table, and balance on one leg with the knee slightly bent. Tighten your stomach muscles to protect your back.

2. Gently swing your other leg forward and backward. Keep your hips still as your leg moves from back to front. Swing up to 20 times on one leg, then swap sides and swing on the other leg.

CAUTION

Never point your toes inwards while exercising – because this can damage your knees.

2

STANDING KNEE LIFT

This exercise mobilizes the quadriceps and the hip flexors at the front of your body.

1. Stand up straight with your left hand on the back of a chair to balance you.

2. Tighten your abdominal muscles.

3. Pull up your right knee so that your foot is parallel to your left knee.

4. Release and repeat on the other leg.

5. Repeat nine more times on each leg.

STANDING LEG CIRCLES

This exercise warms up the buttock muscles by lifting and drawing them together.

1. Stand up straight with good posture and with your knees soft and legs hip-width apart. For balance hold on to the back of a chair.

2. Tighten your abdominal muscles by gently pulling in your navel towards your backbone.

3. Lift your left leg a little way off the foor and gently circle it one way, then the other.

4. Return to the starting position and repeat on the other leg.

5. Repeat nine more times on each leg.

QUAD STRETCH

The quadriceps muscles are found at the front of your thighs and are often referred to as the 'quads'. Depending on how flexible you are, this stretch may feel difficult to do at first.

1. Stand up straight with your feet hip-width apart and your knees soft (slightly bent). Tighten your stomach muscles to protect your back.

2. Bend one leg up behind you and hold your foot or ankle with your hand.

3. Hold for 5 to 10 seconds, then release and repeat on the other side.

4. Repeat twice more on each leg.

HAMSTRING STRETCH

This standing hamstring stretch works the muscles in the back of the thigh.

1. Stand up straight with your knees hip-width apart and your knees soft (slightly bent).

2. Extend one foot forward so that it is pointing in front of you with the weight resting on its heel. Tighten your stomach muscles to protect your back.

3. Rest your hands on the thigh of the bent leg to support your body weight.

4. Bend forward from the hip and feel the stretch in the back of the thigh of the straight leg.

5. Hold for 5 to 10 seconds, then release and repeat on the other side.

6. Repeat twice more on each leg.

FLOOR EXERCISES

INTRODUCTION

In this section you will find basic floor exercises to improve core stability. Many are traditional abdominal exercises or established moves from exercise systems, such as Yoga and Pilates, and offer varying degrees of difficulty. Don't worry if you can't complete the full range of movement suggested in each exercise – as you get fitter, this will become easier.

Establishing good posture makes all the exercises easier to do and more effective. Good posture results from your spine maintaining its natural curve, without sagging. If your posture is incorrect, every movement you make will be inefficient and this could lead to weakness, aching joints and muscles, and an increased risk of injury.

Test your posture by standing on one leg – you should be able to balance without wobbling. Even if you do wobble, the good news is that exercises in this book will naturally improve your posture because they strengthen the major muscles (the core muscles) that support your body.

The basic thing to remember is, if you are standing, imagine your spine is extended beyond your head up towards the sky and that someone is pulling on the end to make you stand to attention, a bit like a puppet on a string. Make sure your shoulders are relaxed – one of the best ways to check is to roll them backwards a few times. This will help you to find their natural resting place.

If an exercise requires you to extend your arms or legs, remember always to keep elbows and knees 'soft' (slightly bent). This will prevent you getting injured.

The correct way to breathe when exercising is to breathe in slowly through your nose (notice how your abdominal cavity rises as you do so) and breathe out slowly through your mouth. Make sure you continue to breathe in and out regularly. Don't hold your breath – this will cause your blood pressure to rise, which can be dangerous.

Right: *Many of the exercises specify keeping your spine in neutral.*

NEUTRAL SPINE

Some exercises will specify using this position as an important part of the exercise. To achieve this, lie down on your back, flat on the floor with your knees slightly bent and feet hip-width apart. Place your thumbs on your bottom ribs and your little fingers on the top of the hip bones. Draw these two points together by gently pulling your navel towards the floor to tighten your abdominal muscles. Keep your back in contact with the floor and do not arch your spine.

TRAIN YOUR BRAIN

Use your mind to help you get the most from your workout. Focus on what you are doing correctly. As you are exercising tell yourself how well you are doing. Think of each muscle contracting and stretching as you do your routine. This can make you do even better, whereas concentrating on what you are doing wrong sets you up to fail. You can even use visualizations to convince yourself that your body is becoming fitter and more toned!

1 HUNDREDS

This is primarily a breathing exercise designed to strengthen the abdominal region. Make sure you don't arch your lower back.

1. Lie on your back with your knees in the air, directly above your hips, making a 90-degree angle with your lower leg. Keep your arms by your sides.

2. Contract your abdominal muscles to lift your shoulders off the floor. In this position, beat your hands up and down while slowly breathing in and out for a count of ten. Perform nine repetitions.

1

TIP

If your abs aren't strong enough to do a complete hundred, rest in between exercises. If you feel any strain in the neck, place one hand behind your head to support it and then alternate arms until you've finished.

2

Dog

2

This classic yoga position strengthens and stretches most of your body. As your flexibility increases you will be able to press your heels into the floor.

1. Start on all fours with your hands under your shoulders and your knees under your hips, hip-distance apart. Keep your spine in neutral and slowly tighten your abdominal muscles.

1

2. Curl your toes under, press back into your palms and, bringing the balls of your feet onto the floor, lift your hips towards the ceiling and straighten your legs until you are forming an inverted 'V' shape.

3. Hold briefly, then come down again on all fours.

4. Perform four repetitions.

YOGA

Many core training exercises come from yoga moves, an ancient form of gentle exercise consisting of body postures and controlled breathing techniques. Yoga is renowned for increasing suppleness of the joints and improving mobility.

2

ROLLING LIKE A BALL

3

This exercise improves your balance and the flexibility of your spine and builds strong abdominal muscles.

1. Sit up with your knees bent and hold your knees with your hands. Pull your abdominal muscles towards your spine to help keep your balance. Tuck your chin into your chest and, staying balanced on your tailbone, lift both feet off the floor.

2. Roll back slowly, bringing your knees closer to your nose until your shoulder blades touch the floor, making sure you do not roll back onto your neck (2a). Then roll forwards to the starting position (2b).

3. Perform three to five repetitions.

1

2a

2b

TIP

Focus on moving from your abdominal muscles rather than letting momentum carry you backwards.

PILATES

This body-conditioning technique focuses on strengthening the core postural muscles to increase your flexibility and mobility.

SWAN

4

This lengthens and strengthens your spine, as well as working your abs. To maintain the tension in your abdominals during this exercise, imagine that you are trying to lift your stomach off the ground.

1. Lie on your front with your arms extended in front of you and your legs extended behind.

2. Keep your spine in neutral and tighten your abdominal muscles. You should feel your pubic bone pressing down into the floor.

3. Raise your shoulders and feet a few centimetres off the ground and hold for a count of ten, then release.

4. Perform two repetitions.

CAUTION

Consult a doctor before doing this exercise if you have ever had any lower-back problems.

VARIATION

Performing this move on an exercise ball strengthens and stretches your back (*see* page 116). If you can feel any discomfort in your lower back, stop immediately. Lie with the ball under your stomach and pelvis. Plant your curled toes on the floor, hip-width apart, and keep your legs straight. Place your hands on the floor, shoulder-width apart. Tighten your abdominal muscles and lift your head so that there is a long line from your head to your heels. Slowly push your pelvis into the ball as you look up and extend your spine away from the ball. Hold for a count of five, then release. Perform three repetitions.

5

SUPINE LEG LIFT

The importance of this exercise is to hold the legs off the floor with correct spinal alignment and abdominal bracing. Use small ankle weights to make this exercise more challenging.

1. Lie on your back with your knees bent and feet on the floor, hip-width apart.

2. Keep your spine and pelvis in neutral and gently tighten your abdominal muscles.

2

TIP
Each leg movement should be slow and controlled.

3. Keeping your knees bent, slowly lift your right leg about 15–20 cm (6–8 in) off the floor and hold the position.

4. Now bring your left leg off the floor and bring it adjacent to the right leg.

5. Slowly lower your right leg back to the floor, then your left leg.

6. Perform six to eight repetitions.

SCISSORS

6

You will feel a stretch in your hamstrings as you perform this exercise, but the main aim is to keep your pelvis, hips and spine still and maintain abdominal tension throughout.

1. Lie on your back with both legs raised, toes pointing to the ceiling and knees slightly bent.

2. Keep your spine in neutral and set (or brace) your abdominal muscles.

2

3

3. Slowly lower your left leg down towards the floor, still keeping your torso in alignment. As your left leg reaches the floor, slowly raise your right leg and continue the movements in a scissoring action.

4. Perform six to eight repetitions on each leg.

TIP

To make this exercise more difficult you can increase the distance over which the legs are lowered, provided you can maintain correct alignment.

7

SIDE LEG LIFT

This exercise is great for strengthening your obliques – the large muscles on the sides of your body that help you to bend or twist your torso. It also strengthens the hips, buttocks and thighs.

1. Lie on your right side with your legs extended but knees soft rather than locked, toes pointed and your right arm supported by a cushion or pillow. Rest your left hand on the floor in front of you and support the side of your head with your right hand.

2. Keep your spine in neutral and set your abdominal muscles.

3. Turn your left leg out slightly, then raise it towards the ceiling as far as Is comfortable. Hold briefly, then slowly release.

4. Perform six to eight repetitions, then repeat on the other side.

SIDE LEG CIRCLES

8

This exercise tones and strengthens your core muscles, as well as the hips, buttocks and inner thighs.

1. Lie on your right side with your head supported by your right hand and your right arm supported by a cushion or pillow. Rest your left hand on the floor in front of you.

2. Bend your right leg in front of you for support.

3. Keep your spine in neutral and set your abdominal muscles.

4. Point your left foot and raise your left leg, raising it as high as feels comfortable. Then draw five small clockwise circles with your toes, keeping your abs strong throughout and moving from your hip joint.

TIP
Keep your torso in line throughout and don't let it sink forwards.

5. Reverse the direction and draw five small anticlockwise circles, then slowly release.

6. Perform six to eight repetitions, then repeat on the other side.

STANDING LEG LIFT

9   2

This will help improve your balance, stabilize the pelvis and tone your thigh and hip muscles. Aim to keep your pelvis stable throughout.

1. Stand with your spine in neutral, feet slightly apart and arms by your sides.

2. Pull your navel in towards your spine and bring your left knee in towards your chest so that your big toe is resting on the side of your right knee. Hold your knee with both hands, keeping your spine straight and your standing leg strong. You will need to drop your left hip down and lift the hip higher on the right side to keep your hips level at this point.

4

3. Hold for a count of three, then release.

4. Repeat with the other leg.

5. Perform four to six repetitions.

VARIATION

To make this exercise more difficult, after step 2 stretch your left leg straight out in front of you at hip height, holding on to the back of your thigh to support it. Release your arms and rest them on your buttocks, but keep your left leg extended in front of you. Hold for up to ten seconds, then lower your leg to the floor and repeat on the other leg. Perform four to six repetitions on each leg.

SIDE STANDING LEG LIFT

10

This works your abdominal muscles and back extensors, as well as your quadriceps, hamstrings and gluteals (buttock muscles).

1. Stand up straight with your spine in neutral, your feet hip-width apart and arms by your sides. Set your abdominal muscles.

2. Support your body weight on your right leg and lift your left leg to the side. As you do this, extend your right arm forwards and your left arm out to the side. Hold for a count of three.

3. Repeat on the other side.

4. Perform six to eight repetitions.

TIP

Add ankle weights for an increased challenge – but only when you can perform the leg lifts perfectly.

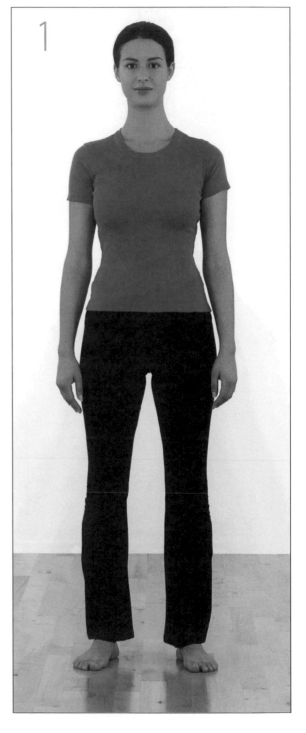

1

2

LUNGE

11

The further you step forwards in this exercise,
the harder your muscles will be worked.

2

1

1. Stand with your hands on your hips
and your feet parallel, hip-width apart.
Brace your abdominal muscles.

2. Take a big step forwards, keeping
your weight evenly balanced between
both legs.

3. Bend both knees as far as is
comfortable so that you lower your torso
down, then return to the starting position.

4. Repeat on the other leg.

5. Perform six to eight repetitions.

3

BASIC SQUAT

12

Keep your spine in neutral and do not allow your pelvis to tilt as you squat down.

1. Start by standing in a level position with your feet parallel and hip-width apart and your hands on your hips. Keep your spine in neutral alignment and tighten your abdominal muscles. Bend your knees as if you're about to sit down.

2. Squat down as far as you can without losing your balance or arching your back.

3. Hold for a count of one, then push through your heels to return to the starting position.

4. Perform six to eight repetitions.

1

SQUAT WITH LEG LIFT

2

This move works your entire lower body. Focus on keeping your abdominal muscles braced to maintain your balance.

1. Stand on the floor with your feet parallel and hip-width apart. Place your hands on your hips, set your abdominal muscles and bend your knees so that you squat back.

2. Press up into a standing position as you simultaneously extend your right leg to the side.

3. Return to the squatting position.

4. Repeat on the other side.

5. Perform six to eight repetitions.

13 LYING HIP ROTATIONS

This exercise tones and strengthens the muscles in the hips, so is great for improving the appearance of the dreaded 'saddlebags' (those annoying pockets of fat that can appear on the outside of the top of the thighs). By clenching your buttocks as you rotate your hip, you'll be giving them a workout, too!

3

1. Lie on your left side, bending your left knee so it's at a 45-degree angle to your body.

2. Lift up and support your upper body with your left arm – this should be a comfortable resting position. Place your right hand on the floor in front of you for additional support.

3. Contract your buttocks and raise your right leg off the floor from the hip joint as far as you can, keeping the foot flexed (bent at the ankle).

4. Gently lower your leg out in front of you, down towards the floor so it's at a right angle to your body. Keep it as straight as you can without locking your knee.

TIP

Try to get your leg as high as you can without straining – you'll find it gets easier with practice.

5. Bring your right leg back into the starting position, keeping it just off the floor.

Number of repetitions: Do three or more repetitions on one side and then reverse the entire movement and do the same on the other.

4

SUPERMAN

14

You need to have a good sense of balance to do this exercise, so if you don't get it right first time, be patient. It's great for increasing core stability and endurance in the joints, as well as working the core muscles in your thighs.

1. Get down on the floor on all fours, then pull in your abdominal muscles.

1

2. Extend your right arm out in front of you and your left leg out behind you, keeping it as straight as you can without locking your elbow or knee. Engage your abdominal muscles to help stop your back from arching – it will reduce any risk of injury. You will feel the muscles working in the thigh of your extended leg. If you want to increase the effects, point your toes – it will make you tense your muscles even harder. Keep your head and neck in line with your back to make sure you're not twisting your neck.

3. Slowly return to the start position and repeat with the opposite leg and arm.

Tip

Do this on soft carpet or a padded exercise mat, so you don't hurt your knees.

Number of repetitions: Beginners should hold the position for 12 seconds, then swap, but if you feel comfortable, try moving your arm and leg in and out for extra toning effects.

2

CRANE STAND

15

This exercise is like the Superman (*see* page 60), but standing up. It's great for working your buttocks, hamstrings and lower back but it does take a lot of skill and balance to achieve, so do it slowly for the best results.

1. Stand on your left leg and take a few seconds to find your balance.

2. Extend your left arm out in front of you and your right leg out behind you. Try to keep your right leg as straight as possible without locking the knee.

2

3. Reach out as far as possible and tilt your body over from the waist so your left arm drops down to the floor.

4. Gently straighten up from the waist so you're back in the starting position. Repeat with the opposite arm and leg. Aim to do around four repetitions, or more if you feel comfortable.

TIP

This exercise is suitable for everyone. Just concentrate and take it slowly to make sure you keep your balance.

3

PLANK

16

This exercise doesn't sound or look too taxing but, if you do it correctly, you'll find that it's one of the most intense exercises in the book, and very effective at toning the abdominal muscles. Many people, especially beginners, find this difficult to hold for long periods of time, so see how you get on. Aim to be able to hold the position for 30 seconds by the end of two weeks.

1. Lie on the floor on your front, resting your forehead on the backs of your hands.

2. Keeping your elbows bent, slide your hands across the floor, rotating from the shoulders, until you find your comfortable 'press-up' position either side of your chest.

3. Curl your toes underneath you and push up off the floor with your hands. Keep your elbows soft to stop them locking, and keep your neck and head relaxed and in line with your spine.

4. Hold the pose for ten seconds, then gently lower yourself back down to the floor again. Remember to breathe during the exercise. Start by doing three sets of ten seconds. Try to increase the time that you hold the Plank to 30 seconds by the end of two weeks.

CAUTION

This exercise can be difficult to do so don't overstrain yourself – you may be able to hold the position for only five seconds at first. Just persevere!

KNEELING BOXED PRESS-UP

17

This exercise targets lots of your upper body and arm muscles so it is great for toning your arms and bust and also for building upper body strength. You will notice the fitter and more toned your arms become, the stronger you will be, and you should soon be able to perform these with ease.

1. Kneel on the mat with your knees directly under your hips. Hands should be slightly wider than shoulder-width apart, with fingers pointing forwards.

2. Keep your body weight over your hands, stomach pulled in tight and your back flat. Slowly lower your body so that your elbows are at a 90-degree angle.

3. Gently push yourself back up to the start position. Aim to perform six to ten repetitions.

1

2

BOXED PRESS-UP (ADVANCED)

As you become fitter, make this exercise a little more challenging by pushing your hips forwards from your knees through to your spine, so that your body is in a straight line. This means that you are now lifting more of your own body weight.

TIP

Keep your stomach muscles pulled in to support your back and, if not using a mat, use a towel to protect your knees on the floor.

BICYCLE

18

This is similar to the Crunches (*see* page 128), but crossing your elbow to the opposite knee targets the obliques instead, which are found at the side of the waist. Practising this exercise will help give you a smaller, more defined middle.

1. Lie on the floor with your knees bent and feet flat on the floor.

2. Rest your hands behind your head and, using your stomach muscles, lift your upper body off the floor, making sure that your lower back stays firmly on the floor.

3

3. Lift your right foot off the floor and bring your right knee towards your chest.

4. Reach forwards and rotate from the waist slightly in order to bring your left elbow towards your right knee. They don't have to touch.

5. Pause for one second, then return to the starting position. Repeat the movement, bringing your right knee towards your left elbow.

6. Continue the exercise on alternate sides for 30 seconds. Aim to do as many repetitions as you can in 30 seconds – around 12. Take a brief pause if you have to, for example, between sets of six.

TIP

Make sure your head and neck are in line with your spine and that you're looking up towards the ceiling – it will prevent you from straining your neck.

4

BICEP CURL

19

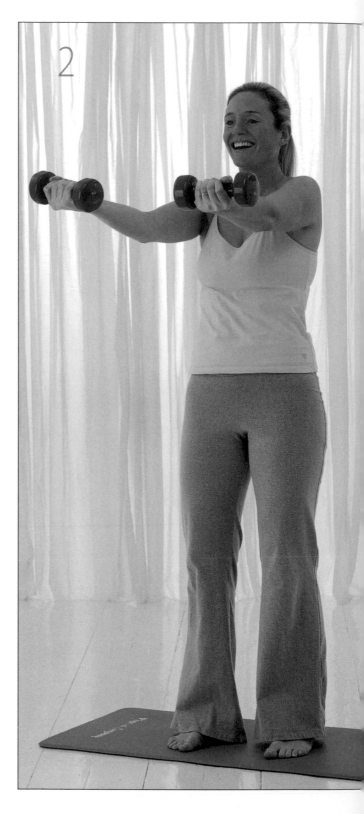

The biceps are the muscles at the front of the upper arms. They are relatively easy to tone, so practising this exercise will help give you shapely arms that you'll want to show off.

1. Stand up tall with feet hip-width apart and knees soft.

2. Extend your arms out in front of you with palms facing upwards, holding a tin of soup or a dumb-bell in each hand.

3. Bend your elbows and bring both your hands in towards your shoulders so that your arms form right-angles.

4. Reverse the movement so that your elbows are fully extended in front of you again. Keep your elbows soft at all times.

5. Repeat the movement for 30 seconds. Aim to do as many repetitions as you can without rushing.

TRICEP EXTENSION

20

The triceps are the muscles at the back of the upper arms. If they're left to slack, it can lead to the dreaded 'bingo-wing' effect, where loose skin on the underside of your arm wobbles as you wave. It's classically a hard muscle to target, but this exercise will help to tighten and tone.

1. Stand with your feet hip-width apart. Pick up a heavy object with both hands – choose something that you can work comfortably with, such as a dumb-bell or a heavy book.

2. Bring the object over your head with straight arms.

3. Bend your arms at the elbows, so you slowly lower it down between your shoulder blades.

4. Reverse the movement by straightening your arms so you bring the object directly back above your head.

5. Repeat Steps 3 and 4 slowly, so you're in control of the movement. Aim to do around seven repetitions in 30 seconds.

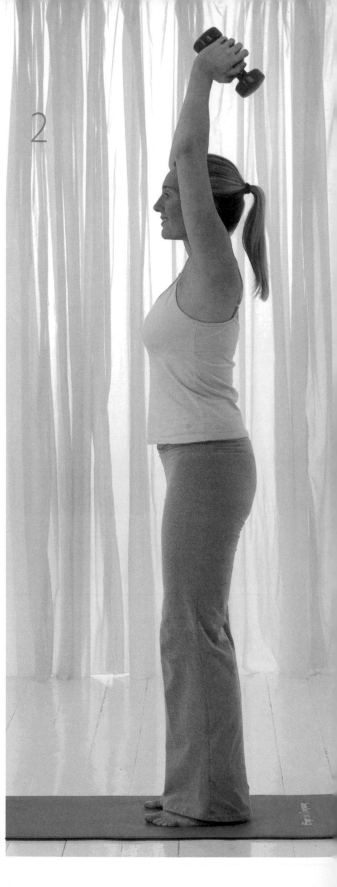

2

3

TIP
Choose a weight that's challenging but not so heavy that you can't control it – you don't want to end up dropping it on your head.

21 TRICEP KICK BACK

This exercise isolates the back of the upper arms, specifically targeting the troublesome area sometimes referred to as 'auntie's arms' or 'bingo-wings'.

1. Kneel over a chair, with one arm supporting your body and one knee bent on the chair. Ensure that the elbow of the supporting arm stays soft and that the knee of the leg extended to the floor is also soft.

2. With a weight in one hand, position your upper arm so it is parallel to the floor and bent at the elbow.

3. Slowly extend the arm until it is straight, then slowly return and repeat. Do all your repetitions and then repeat on the other arm, by turning around and placing your opposite leg on the chair.

2

TIP

For a greater range of motion, the upper arm can be positioned with the elbow at a slightly higher angle than the shoulder.

3

BENCH DIP

22

As well as working your triceps, this will help improve your core stability and tone up your tummy. It's especially great for the arms because you're using your body weight to strengthen and tone.

2

1. Sit on the edge of a sturdy chair with your hands resting either side of your bottom, gripping the edge of the seat.

2. Walk your feet away from the chair as far as you can, so your bottom comes off the edge of the chair.

3. Letting your arms take your body weight, bend your elbows and, with knees bent, slowly lower your body towards the floor – make sure you don't end up sitting on the floor; hovering just above the floor is the ideal position. Make sure your weight is evenly distributed so you don't topple the chair.

4. Straighten your arms, so you bring your lower body back up. Repeat Steps 3 and 4. Aim for around six repetitions.

TIP
Keep your forearms vertical at all times – it will help to reduce the amount of strain on your shoulders.

CIRCLES IN THE AIR

23

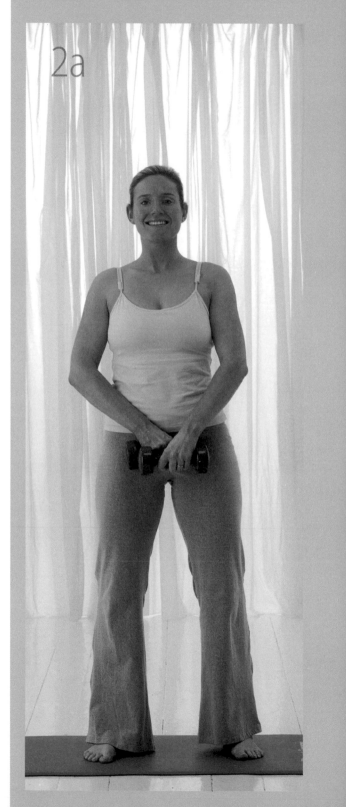

2a

This exercise is great for general toning of the arms and shoulders. Using weights will also help to develop strength in the arms and have a pumping effect on the muscles, so you'll look great in short-sleeved tops.

1. Stand with your feet hip-width apart, knees slightly bent and arms resting by your sides.

2. With a dumb-bell in each hand (2a), cross your arms in front of each other (2b) level with your hips, then circle them up towards the ceiling so they cross over in the air above your head (2c). Then bring them back round to the starting position.

3. Pause for one second, then repeat the movement in the opposite direction. Aim to do around 15 repetitions in 30 seconds.

TIP

Keep your arms fully extended as you circle them so you are working as many muscles as possible, but remember to keep your elbows soft.

REVERSE SIT-UP

24

This is a great exercise for strengthening the lower back. Adding an arm rotation to the move delivers a double toning boost to the shoulders.

1. Lie flat and face down on the floor with your forehead resting on the backs of your hands.

2. Squeeze your buttocks and use your stomach muscles to raise your chest off the floor as far as you feel comfortable.

3. Squeeze your shoulder blades together by rotating your arms around from the shoulders, so your palms are facing downwards and your forearms are hovering at chest level. This will help to give the shoulders a workout, too.

4. Return your arms to the starting position and lower your chest back down to the floor. Repeat the movement. Aim to do around 15 or more repetitions in 30 seconds.

CAUTION

Don't try to pull your chest back too far or it will force your lower back to arch and put a strain on the muscles. Just do what feels comfortable.

25

MOY COMPLEX

This exercise is also known as the 'row, rotate and press' and is a great way to tone the muscles in your back, without having to use the complicated machinery that you find in the gym.

TIP

Remember to relax your head and neck and keep them in line with your spine, so you don't strain any muscles.

2

1. Sit on the edge of a chair with a dumb-bell or tin of soup in each hand.

2. Bend over from the waist so your chest is resting on your knees. Make sure your head and neck are relaxed, so that you're looking down towards the floor.

3. Start with your hands resting on the floor, with elbows slightly bent, then bend your arms and bring your hands up to shoulder level.

4. Rotate your wrists and extend your arms out in front of you so that they're parallel to the floor.

5. Retrace your steps so you're back in the Step 2 position, then repeat the movement. Aim to do around 15 repetitions in 30 seconds.

4

SUPER CHEST TONER

26

This is a great exercise to work deep into the chest muscles, which can help to support and lift the bust muscles, as well as increase your range of flexibility through your shoulders.

1. Lie on the mat, face up, with your knees bent and feet firmly on the floor.

2. Using a weight in each hand, bend your arms out to the sides so that they rest on the floor, elbows in line with your shoulders and bent to form an L-shape.

3. Slowly lift your arms off the floor while maintaining the bend and aim to bring both arms to meet directly in line with your face. Hold for a couple of seconds, then slowly lower back to the floor and repeat.

TIP
By keeping your navel pulled down tight to your spine, you will protect your back throughout this workout. Doing this will also tone your deepest abdominal muscles.

CHEST PRESS

27

This exercise targets two muscles – your triceps and your chest muscle. This is a great exercise for women as it tightens the muscles that support your bust, giving you a good bust lift.

1. Stand with good upright posture, knees soft and your feet hip-width apart.

2. Using a weight in each hand, bend your arms so your hands are in front of your shoulders.

TIP
Focus on engaging your abdominal muscles by pulling your navel tight to your spine. This helps protect your back.

2

3

3. Gently extend your arms straight out, keeping them at shoulder height.

4. Hold for a second when your arms are fully extended. Slowly return your arms to the start position. Perform six to ten repetitions.

BASIC OBLIQUE CURL

28

Twisting curls work your rectus abdominis muscles and the obliques, the muscles that give definition to the waist. These exercises will tighten your stomach muscles and trim your waist.

1. Lie on your back with your knees bent, feet flat on the floor and hip-width apart. Put your hands by your temples at the sides of your head. Lift your left leg and rest the ankle of that leg across your right thigh – this will turn your supported left leg out slightly. Keep your spine in neutral and tighten your abdominal muscles.

2. Curl up, rotating your trunk to the left and breathing out as you do so. Your right elbow should be moving towards your left knee. Keep your left side in contact with the floor to help support your back.

3. Curl back down again, breathing in as you do so.

4. Repeat this exercise to the other side, using the other leg.

CAUTION

Avoid this exercise if you have neck problems.

NECK SUPPORT

Some may complain of neck pain when starting abdominal work. This is usually because you are using the neck muscles rather than the abdominal muscles to lift your head and shoulders. One solution is to place a towel behind your head and hold both ends taut so it supports your neck while you are curling up.

2

SLIGHTLY HARDER OBLIQUE CURL

1. Lie on your back with your spine in neutral, your knees bent and your feet flat on the floor, hip-width apart. Put your right hand by your temple at the side of your head. Lift your left leg and rest the ankle of that leg on your right knee. Wrap your left hand around the inside of your left thigh and press your thigh outwards.

2. Breathe in and tighten your abdominal muscles. Breathe out as you curl up and across, to bring your right elbow towards your left knee.

3. Curl back down again, breathing in as you do so, then cross over your right leg and work the other side.

1

RESISTANCE BAND

INTRODUCTION

Resistance-band training offers a number of benefits, and in this chapter you will learn how and why resistance bands work simply and effectively. You will discover the fundamental principles of exercise as practised by top sports people and dancers. You will learn how you can maintain your consistency with exercise and enjoy the thrill of knowing that resistance-band exercises can change your body, motivating you to reach your desired goal.

Resistance-band training is simple: the more the elastic band is stretched, the more the resistance increases, and likewise, the band will contract as the force decreases. Neither type of elastic resistance relies on gravity, unlike most exercise machines and classic free weights, such as the dumb-bell. Instead, resistance is dependent upon how far the resistance band is stretched, and continuously and increasingly places demands on your muscles as it contracts throughout the whole range of motion.

Both bands and tubing come in different lengths and many resistance levels. The bands or tubes are colour-coded according to their resistance levels. Different manufacturers use different colour schemes for their bands and tubes, but generally both the colour and resistance of the band or tube start light and progress through to darker colours, which represent increased resistance.

SAFETY ADVICE

- Seek approval from your medical adviser before undertaking resistance exercises, particularly if you have any existing musculoskeletal problems.
- Use latex-free products if you have a latex allergy.
- Always warm up before exercise, and cool down afterwards.
- Maintain correct posture at all times.
- If you feel any pain during exercise, stop immediately.
- Never point a band under tension towards your face.
- Protect the resistance band from sharp objects.

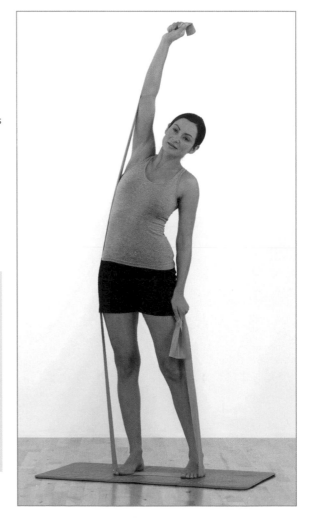

Right: *It is important to maintain good posture when exercising.*

Above: *Resistance bands let you move more freely and achieve a greater range of motion than resistance machines. Greater resistance can be achieved by adjusting your angle of movement.*

Below: *There are many elastic-band resistance products available; most are basically resistance bands or resistance tubes to which handles may be attached.*

29 OVER SHOULDER PRESS

This exercise targets your shoulders, helping to improve your ability to lift or push. It also increases your strength when reaching overhead.

1. Stand with the middle of the band under your right foot. If using handles, ensure they are securely attached to the ends of the resistance band, although handles are not essential. Keep your feet shoulder-width apart, but with the left foot slightly in front, and your knees slightly bent (known as soft knees). Hold the ends of the band at shoulder level.

CAUTION

If you experience shoulder pain during this exercise, stop and reassess your technique and the resistance of the band. Try using a band with less resistance. If pain persists, consult your health professional.

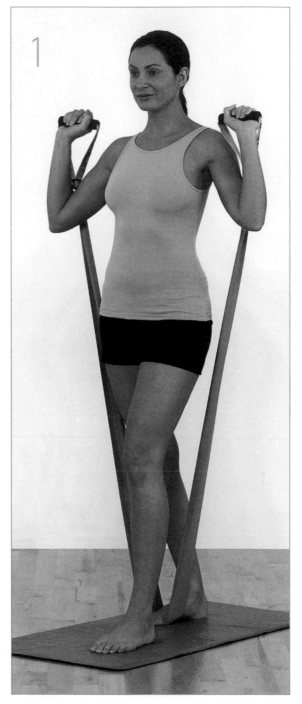

2

2. Lift your hands above your head, straightening your elbows. Hold this position for a count of one, then return your hands to shoulder height slowly and with control.

3. Reverse your position to work the left side.

VARIATION

To initiate your core stability, perform the exercise while standing on one leg, and for an additional challenge place a foam- or air-filled stability pad under that foot. Alternate the leg you stand on during core stability, completing half your repetitions on each leg.

SHOULDER LATERAL RAISE

30

This is an intensive exercise for your shoulders. It can also help to improve your reach out to the sides, a movement that is essential in many sports.

1. Stand with the middle of the band under your right foot. Holding one end of the band in each hand, start with both arms extended down by your sides.

2. Keeping your thumbs upwards, lift both arms outwards and upwards slowly and with control, keeping your elbows straight. Stop for a count of one at shoulder level, then return your arms back to the start position.

TIP

Avoid shrugging your shoulders by keeping your shoulder blades down; maintain a straight back and remember to breathe normally throughout the exercise. Exhale slowly as you apply tension and inhale through the return phase.

VARIATIONS

Take your arms completely over your head, again keeping your thumbs upwards. To work your core stability, perform the exercise standing on one leg, and for an additional challenge place a foam- or air-filled stability pad under that foot. Alternate the leg you stand on during core stability, completing half your repetitions on each leg.

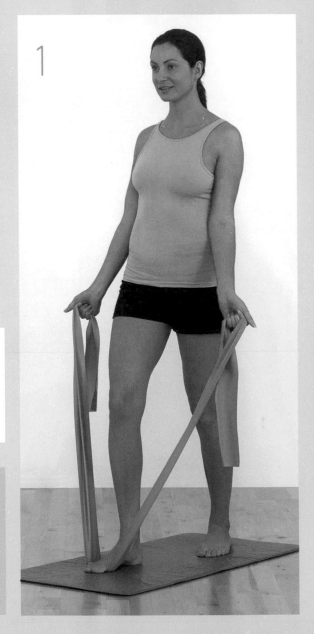

1

2

PUSH-UP

31

A simply wonderful exercise for strengthening your chest, upper arms, back and core muscles.

TIP

This exercise can be performed while kneeling to reduce the tension, enabling more repetitions.

1. Lie chest-down on the floor. Pass the resistance band across your back and wrap it around both hands so that you can place your palms flat on the floor at shoulder level, and slightly more than shoulder-width apart. Make sure the band is taut. Stretch out your legs with your feet together. Look slightly forwards rather than at the floor, so that you are resting on your chin rather than your nose. Make sure your core muscles are activated by sucking in your stomach while exhaling, and when you feel your stomach muscles contract, lock them into this contracted position and continue to breathe normally.

2. Straighten your arms, pushing your body off the floor slowly as you exhale steadily. Keep your upper and lower back straight, correcting any arching. Hold this position for a count of one, then release very slowly to the start position, inhaling all the way.

TARGET HEART RATE

Are you training within your target heart rate? Time your heartbeat for 15 seconds. Multiply the number of beats over 15 seconds by four. This will give you your beats per minute.

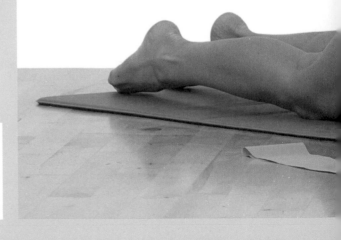

SIDE BEND

32

The side bend helps to encourage a good posture. Control your technique with a smooth motion. There is no rush.

1. Stand on the middle of the resistance band with your feet shoulder-width apart. Keep your knees and hips slightly bent and your back straight, and make sure the band is secure. Hold one end of the resistance band in each hand.

VARIATION

You can work your core by standing on your right leg, with one end of the resistance band secured beneath your foot. Hold the other end of the band in your right hand, letting your left hand rest by your side. Extend your right arm high above your head with a slightly bent elbow that you lock into this position, and then extend your left arm down by your side. Lean your trunk towards the left, stretching the band with your right hand. Hold the end position for a count of one, then return to the start position slowly and with control.

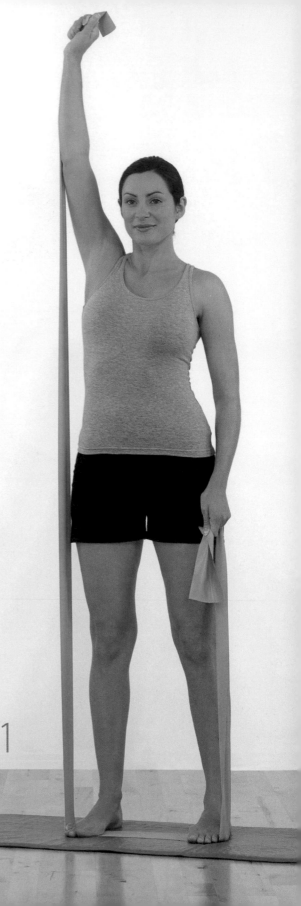

1

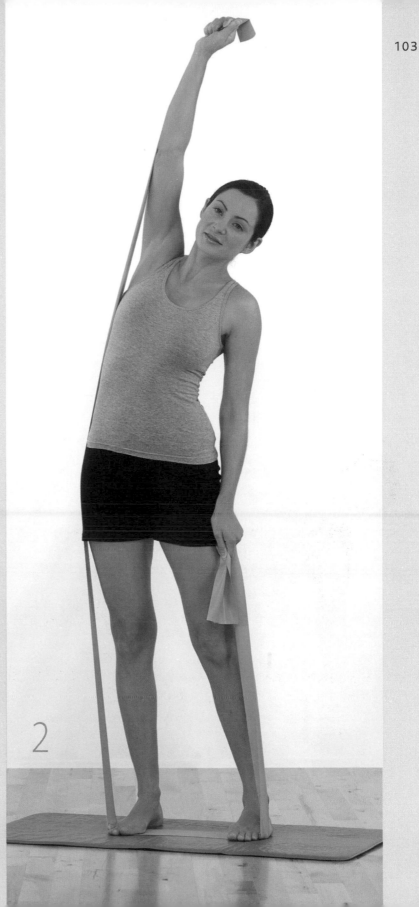

2. Extend your right arm high above your head with a slightly bent elbow that you lock into this position, and extend your left arm down by your side. Lean your trunk towards the left, stretching the band with your right hand. Hold the end position for a count of one, then return to the start position slowly and with control.

3. Reverse your position to work the opposite side.

2

SIDE BRIDGE

33

This exercise is difficult, but good for toning the abdominals and the muscles in the side of your trunk.

1. Wrap the resistance band around your lower legs, just below your knees. Make sure the band is taut and tie the ends. Lie on your right side on the floor, using a padded mat for additional comfort. Bend your right elbow under your right shoulder, propping yourself up off the floor.

2

SIDE BRIDGE | 105

2. Activate your core muscles by sucking in your stomach while exhaling, and, when you feel your stomach muscles contract, lock them into this contracted position and continue to breathe normally. Keeping your knees bent, lift your hips up off the floor, maintaining a straight back.

3. Holding this position, separate your knees, causing the resistance band to stretch. Hold this position for a count of one, then return to the start position slowly and with control.

4. Reverse your position to work the opposite side.

VISUALIZATION

Visualizing before actually executing the techniques assists your ability to carry out the exercise correctly. Perform the technique through your eyes, adding feeling. When you visualize, ensure your technique is absolutely perfect. Practise your visualizing when exercising, then expand it into other areas of your training.

3

HIP ABDUCTION

34

This intense exercise is very effective at toning the abdominals and the muscles in the rear and sides of your hip.

1. Sit on the floor with your legs extended and your knees slightly bent; use a padded floor mat for additional comfort. Loop the resistance band around both legs, just above your ankles, and tie the ends of the band together. Lean back onto your elbows in a reclined position.

TIP

This is a strenuous exercise. Rest with your legs on the floor in between alternating the 'working' leg.

3

2. Activate your core muscles by sucking in your stomach while exhaling, and, when you feel your stomach muscles contract, lock them into this contracted position and continue to breathe normally.

3. Lift both legs off the floor by approximately 10–15 cm (4–6 in).

4. Maintaining your right leg in this position, draw your left leg out to the side, still 10–15 cm (4–6 in) off the floor. Hold this outwards draw for a count of one, then slowly release.

5. Repeat, drawing out the right leg.

CAUTION

Never hold your breath when stretching or exercising. Exhaling after a deep breath enables you to release muscle tension in your body. This enables the muscles to relax more and therefore increases their length.

LEG PRESS

35

Strengthening your thigh and buttock muscles can help you in many sports, including running, surfing, windsurfing and jumping.

1. Lie on your back with both knees bent; use a padded mat for additional comfort. Loop the middle of the resistance band under your left foot, clasping one end of the band in each hand.

2

2. Keeping your right foot flat on the floor, flex your left hip, raising your left foot and keeping your left knee bent. Ensure the resistance band is taut – adjust your grip on the band to increase or decrease tension.

3. Keeping your back straight and flat on the floor, slowly extend your left knee until your leg is straight. Hold this position for a count of one, then release to the start position slowly and with control.

4. Reverse your position to work the opposite side.

ACTIVATING YOUR CORE

Activate your core muscles by sucking in your stomach while exhaling, and, when you feel your stomach muscles contract, lock them into this contracted position and continue to breathe normally.

3

ANKLE PLANTERFLEXION

36

This is an excellent ankle exercise, working all the muscles in your lower leg that assist in pushing your foot downwards.

1. Sit on the floor with your legs extended, using a padded mat for additional comfort. Loop the middle of the resistance band under your right foot and clasp one end of the band in each hand.

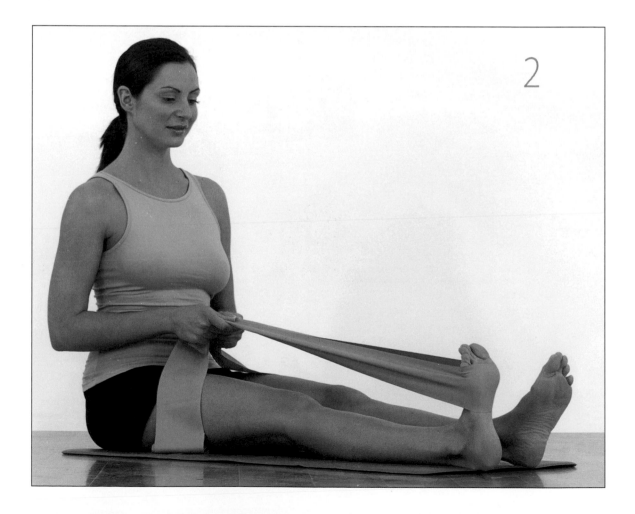

2

3

2. Start with your right ankle flexed, making sure the resistance band is taut. If necessary, adjust your grip on the band, increasing or decreasing the tension accordingly.

3. Extend your ankle away from your head against the resistance band. Hold your ankle in full extension for a count of one, then slowly return your foot to the start position.

4. Reverse your position to work the opposite side.

ROLL-UP

37

This exercise stretches the spine and builds deep abdominal strength. Make sure you roll down on a soft surface, such as an exercise mat.

1. Sit up straight with your legs extended in front of you, knees bent. Your feet should be parallel and close together. Place the wide part of a resistance band or towel around the balls of your feet and hold the ends of the band. Keep your spine in neutral and tighten your abdominal muscles.

2. Tip your pelvis backwards and begin to roll back until your shoulders touch the floor.

3. Release your neck, head and arms, letting them down onto the floor.

4. Reverse the movement, rolling back up to a sitting position.

5. Perform six to eight repetitions.

EXERCISE BALL

INTRODUCTION

Exercises that use a ball work on your body's muscle groups from a strong, central core, using good breathing techniques, strong mental focus and smooth, flowing movements throughout. It's an intelligent workout that combines the best elements of Western and Eastern exercise disciplines – muscle tone, strength and intensity of movement with relaxation techniques and mind-body connections. It's an extremely safe, holistic, non-stressful and effective way to work out and can be performed almost anywhere, any time, because the equipment is light, hardwearing, portable and cheap. Working out with an exercise ball is also fun.

Exercising with a ball is one of he best ways there is to improve the way your body looks, feels and works, because it gives both your mind and your body a good workout. It works on all aspects of your body – bones, muscles, ligaments and joints. By training your mind to exert a greater influence over your body, you can direct your energy towards what you want to achieve with positive thinking.

The whole point about using an exercise ball is that it is an unstable base, which makes you work extra muscles and develop new skills – the simple act of sitting on the ball improves postural strength and awareness. Your abdominal and spinal muscles, which act as a splint around your spine, will become stronger, and you will also learn exercises to help strengthen and protect your back. Over time, your movements will become more fluid and graceful, and of course your fitness, strength and stamina will all improve.

As an added bonus, using a ball improves your balance and fine-tunes motor (or movement) skills. Ball-based exercises are also excellent for reducing stress – stretching encourages greater relaxation, particularly when combined with mental focus and a good breathing technique.

Nearly everyone can benefit from working out on an exercise ball, whatever their level of fitness. Even if you haven't exercised for years, or have recently had a baby, you can start by doing a few stretches and bounces, and make your workout harder as your strength improves.

MENTAL FOCUS

To feel the full benefit of exercising using a ball, you need to approach each exercise with good mental focus. By concentrating on how and where you are moving, you are more likely to move correctly and safely and become aware of the way your body is responding. Using your mind and your emotions will help you to get the most out of your workout. Use positive thoughts – tell yourself that you are doing well and can do even better. Use visualizations to get yourself into the right frame of mind. Visualize somewhere beautiful and peaceful, such as a mountain, garden or beach, and picture yourself there. Breath slowly and rhythmically as you do so while repeating positive affirmations, such as 'my arm muscles are becoming toned'.

CHOOSING THE RIGHT BALL

The only equipment you need for your exercise ball workout is the right sized ball and a mat or towel, or a padded surface, to protect your spine and prevent bruising. It's worth buying a proper sports mat if you can. If you wish, you can also work up to using hand and ankle weights when you feel ready to try more advanced exercises.

Exercise balls are widely available from sports shops and are not expensive. There are many exercise balls on the market, varying in colour, size, cost and quality. Be sure to choose one that is burst-resistant and designed to take at least 300kg (660lb) in weight (remember that the ball will have to take the combined weight of your body and any weights you may be using). Burst-resistant balls are much safer and stronger, and more likely to maintain their shape. If you accidentally roll over a sharp object, they will deflate gradually rather than explode. Cheaper balls are often shiny and slippery, making them less safe.

Choosing the right size of ball

When you are sitting on your ball, your knees and hips should be at an angle of 90 degrees or more. Using a ball that is too small or too large makes exercising awkward. The length of your arm from the shoulder to the fingertip is generally a good way to work out which is the right ball for you, but try one out in the shop to make sure.

Arm length	Ball size required
56–65cm (22–25½in)	55cm (21½in)
66–80cm (26–31½in)	65cm (25½in)
81–90cm (32–35½in)	75cm (29½in)
more than 90cm (35½in)	85cm (33½in)

Inflate your ball according to the manufacturer's instructions using a hand-operated pump so that it is firm, with a little give, but not tight like a drum. A slightly firmer ball makes it harder to stabilize and balance.

STAYING SAFE

• Start every exercise near something you can hold on to – this is essential if your balance is less than perfect or you are pregnant.
• Never attempt any exercise you think you cannot manage.
• Stop if you feel tired, ill or very out of breath.
• Keep long hair tied back.

Exercise area

Choose a safe, non-slip area to exercise on. Your surroundings should be free of furniture and clutter. Check the floor for sharp objects, which could hurt you or damage the exercise ball. If possible, try to exercise in front of a full-length mirror so that you can check what you are doing and correct your position when necessary.

THE BRIDGE

38

The bridge is used as the starting position in many exercises, so it's important to be able to do this one properly. It works the abdominal muscles, lower back, pelvic stabilizers, gluteals and hamstrings. When exercising, always keep your spine in neutral and do not let your back arch. Keep the ball as still as possible throughout.

BASIC BRIDGE

This basic exercise is suitable for beginners.

1. Lie on your back with your arms by your sides. Place your feet on the ball so that it is resting under your calf muscles. Tighten your abdominal muscles.

2. Lift your hips off the floor using your buttock muscles, until your body is diagonal from shoulders to knees.

2

BRIDGE WITH LEG LIFTS

Suitable for beginners, this exercise involves lifting one leg from the ball. This strengthens the muscles at the back of the buttocks and thighs, while increasing balance and control in the stabilizing muscle groups.

1. Lie on your back with your arms by your sides. Place your feet on the ball so that the ball is resting under your calf muscles. Tighten your abdominal muscles.

2. Lift your hips off the floor using your buttock muscles, until your body is diagonal from shoulders to knees.

3. Slowly raise one leg from the ball and hold for a count of five.

4. Return to the ball and repeat using the other leg.

HIGH BRIDGE

An intermediate exercise, the High Bridge is suitable for those who have mastered the easier Bridge exercises.

1. Lie on your back with your arms by your sides and your knees bent. Place your feet on top of the ball.

2. Tighten your abdominal muscles and slowly lift your hips from the floor using your buttock muscles, keeping your knees bent and feet on the ball until your body is diagonal from knees to shoulders.

3. Hold for a count of five, then return to the start position and repeat.

REVERSE BRIDGE

39

This is the starting point for many exercises and you need to be able to perform it correctly to work out safely. It works the abdominal muscles, lower back, pelvic stabilizers, gluteals and hamstrings while improving your balance. Keep your spine in neutral throughout and do not let your back sag or arch. Keep the ball as still as possible. These exercises are suitable for beginners.

ROLLING IN AND OUT OF REVERSE BRIDGE

1. Sit on the ball with your hands by your sides and your feet hip-width apart.

2. To move into reverse bridge, walk your feet forwards, rolling your hips down and lying back on the ball as you do so. Stop when your shoulder blades are on the ball. Your knees should be bent at a 90-degree angle, and your abdominal muscles tight.

3. Lower your head to the ball and lift your hips.

4. Hold for a count of five. To make this harder, bring your feet together.

5. Drop your hips again and lift your head off the ball.

6. Slowly walk your feet back, pressing your lower back into the ball as you go, and return to the starting position.

3

REVERSE BRIDGE WITH LEG EXTENSION

1. Lie with the ball under your shoulders and your feet, hip-width apart, in the reverse bridge position.

2. Tighten your abdominal muscles and lift one leg away from the floor, keeping your knee bent.

3. Hold for a count of five, then return to the starting position.

4. Repeat using the other leg.

TIP

If your head is hanging back over the ball, walk further forwards. If your chin is on your chest, walk back a little.

2

BASIC ABDOMINALS

40

These exercises focus on giving a good workout to the muscles which support and strengthen your lower spine, as well as playing an important part in keeping your pelvis stable. Try to keep your pelvis in neutral and do not pull up your tailbone.

PREPARATION FOR ABDOMINALS

This will prepare you for the more difficult abdominal exercises.

1. Place the ball against a wall.

2. Lie on the floor with your feet on the ball and your knees bent. Place a folded towel or small cushion between your thighs.

3. Very gently, breathe in through your nose. As you breathe out, feel your stomach muscles pulling down to the floor.

4. Hold for a count of four. Squeeze the towel or cushion with your thighs. This will contract your deep internal muscles.

BASIC ABDOMINALS

1. Lie on the floor with your feet on the ball, with your knees bent and legs together.

2. Place your hands on your hip bones to stabilize your pelvis.

3. Very gently, breathe in and let your knees fall open to hip-width apart.

4. As you breathe out, bring your legs back together, pulling your stomach in so that your navel is being drawn down and into your spine.

ABDOMINALS

41

In addition to strengthening the abdominal muscles, abdominal exercises will teach you how to curl your upper body while keeping your spine in alignment.

2

1. Sit on the ball with feet hip-width apart.

2. Lean backwards, moving the ball forwards with your pelvis. Stretch your arms out in front of you to keep your balance.

3. When you feel the lower abdominal muscles tighten, hold for a count of five, then return to a seated position by pulling in the pelvis.

4. To make the exercise harder, try holding the position for longer periods. You could also cross your arms over your chest.

4

CRUNCHES

42

2

Putting your feet on the ball increases the stabilizing ability of your abdominal muscles. It also makes your abdominal muscles work a little harder than in the previous exercise.

BASIC CRUNCHES

1. Lie on your back with both heels resting on the ball, your hips and knees at an angle and your arms resting on the floor.

2. Tighten your abdominal muscles and breathe steadily.

3. Begin to nod your chin while your head is still on the floor.

4. Lift your head, bending the upper body and raising your arms parallel to the floor. Use your abdominal muscles, not your hands, to lift your head.

5. Hold for a count of four. You should be looking at your thighs, not the ceiling.

6. Return your head and arms to the floor.

4

CAUTION

When lying on your back you need to make sure your head is not tilted, making your neck arch. Drop your chin gently forwards instead.

INTERMEDIATE CRUNCHES

1. Lie on your back. Grasp the ball under your knees and lift it from the floor.

2. Tighten your abdominal muscles and put your hands either side of your head.

3. Slowly lift your shoulders from the floor towards your knees.

4. Hold for a count of five and roll your shoulders back down to the start position.

ADVANCED CRUNCHES

1. Lie on your back. Grasp the ball underneath your calves and lift them from the floor to an angle of about 45 degrees.

2. Tighten your abdominal muscles and put your hands either side of your head.

3. Hold this position, and slowly lift your shoulders from the floor towards your knees.

4. Hold for a count of five, then roll your shoulders back down to the floor, keeping your legs raised.

HIP CIRCLES

43

Poor posture – caused, for example, by spending long periods of time hunched over a computer – compresses the backbones, causing pain and misalignment. This exercise will release your back and stretch out your shoulders to increase spinal mobility so that you can avoid back strain.

1. Sit on the ball with your feet shoulder-width apart and your hands touching the ball on either side.

2. Tighten your abdominal muscles and use your pelvis to rotate the ball slowly three times to the right in small clockwise circles.

3. Repeat on the other side.

CAUTION

If you feel your neck crunching, you've taken it too far back.

1

FOOT KICKS

44

This exercise helps to tone and stretch your legs and act as a gentle warm up for more difficult exercises. It also promotes strength and mobility in your spine and stabilizing pelvic muscles. Adding arm to leg movements challenges your balance and coordination. Tighten your abdominal muscles throughout.

1. Sit on the ball with your feet slightly wider than hip-width apart and flat on the floor and your arms hanging loosely by your sides.

2. Hold your arms out at chest level to help you balance. Tighten your abdominal muscles and keep your back straight.

3. Kick your right foot up until the knee is as straight as possible.

4. Return the foot to the floor and repeat with the left leg.

5. Repeat the whole exercise, but this time, when kicking up a leg, swing the opposite arm upwards.

6. To make this exercise more difficult, use ankle weights.

TIP

If you lift your feet too high you will lose your balance.

3

BEND AND STRETCH

This intermediate exercise makes your deep stabilizing muscles work to control the weight and movements of your legs. It also strengthens the inner thigh muscles and those that control side bending of the lower spine.

1. Lie on your back with your knees bent.

2. Pick up the ball between your ankles and squeeze together, pulling your knees towards you.

3. Sit up far enough to rest your upper body on your elbows.

4. Straighten your legs out diagonally and hold for a count of five.

5. Return to the starting position.

HIP FLEXIONS

These exercises focus on working the hip muscles, which play a very important part in stabilizing your pelvis and supporting your lower back, as well as keeping the hip joints flexible. Make sure you keep your spine in neutral alignment throughout the exercise.

HIP FLEXIONS FOR BEGINNERS

1. Lie with the ball under your stomach.

2. Keeping yourself supported on your straightened arms, roll forwards until the ball is under your shins.

3. Tighten your abdominal muscles and keep your spine straight. Then slowly bring your knees towards your chest, rolling the ball forwards with you.

4. Hold for a count of three, then stretch out your legs to return to the starting position.

HIP EXTENSIONS

1. Kneel on the floor with the ball under your stomach.

2. Tighten your abdominal muscles and slowly extend your left leg and right arm until they are horizontal. Keep your toes pointing towards the floor.

3. Hold for a count of five and return to the starting position.

4. Repeat using the other leg and arm.

ADVANCED HIP EXTENSIONS

1. Put on ankle weights and lie prone on the ball so that it is under your pelvis and stomach.

2. Lift your left leg, bend the knee and push your foot up towards the ceiling. This should lift your thigh away from the ball.

3. Hold for a count of five, then slowly return to the starting position.

4. Repeat on the other side.

BOTTOM TONER

47

The following exercise will tone and stretch your buttock muscles. Buttock muscles are not just for sitting on – they also help move your legs. Tension in the gluteals can lead to back problems and poor posture so it's very important to keep these muscles flexible and strong.

BASIC BOTTOM TONER

1. Lie on your front with the ball between your ribs and your hips. Your arms should be shoulder-width apart with the palms of your hands planted on the floor. Your toes should be touching the floor with your feet flexed for balance.

2. Slowly lift your left leg until it is pointing out straight behind you, keeping the buttock muscles clenched as you do so.

3. Hold for a count of five.

4. Return to the starting position and repeat on the other side.

1

BOTTOM TONER

1. Lie on your front with the ball between your ribs and your hips. Your arms should be shoulder-width apart with the palms of your hands planted on the floor. Your toes should be touching the floor with your feet flexed for balance.

2. Slowly lift both legs up, keeping your buttock muscles clenched as you do so.

3. Hold for a count of five, then return to the starting position.

WALL PUSH-UP

48

Using the ball means that all your body's muscles are worked to maintain balance and keep the spine in neutral, rather than just the shoulder and arm muscles. Make sure you work at a distance from the ball where you can maintain good control and spinal position. If your upper back is arching or your lower back swaying, step your hands back to shorten the distance between you and the ball.

1. Stand holding the ball at chest height between you and the wall.

2. Roll the ball up to shoulder height.

3. Holding the ball against the wall, step back and keep your feet hip-width apart. Keep your body in a straight line from your shoulders to your heels.

4. Slowly bend your elbows outwards to move your chest towards the wall.

5. Hold for a count of two, then press back away from the wall to straighten your arms.

6. To make this harder, press up with one hand only, placing the other behind your back.

CAUTION

Do not do these exercises if you have a shoulder, neck or back problem.

3

SHOULDER PRESS

49

It is important to stretch out your shoulders after performing upper body strengthening exercises. This exercise works the levator scapulae at the back and sides of the neck, which lift the shoulders, and will improve flexibility in your shoulder joints and release tension in your chest muscles.

1

2

1. Sit on the ball with your feet hip-width apart. Keep your arms bent with your elbows at shoulder level, holding small weights.

2. Tighten your abdominal muscles. Slowly press the weights upwards and towards each other until they are touching, with your arms fully extended.

3. Slowly lower the weights to the starting position, bringing your elbows slightly backwards and drawing your shoulder blades together.

4. To make this harder, raise alternate legs as you press the weights.

4

CAUTION

Avoid these exercises if you have any shoulder or neck pain.

CHEST PRESS

50

This exercise works on the pectorals – the chest muscles – and will also benefit the upper back, mid-back and arm muscles.

1. Lie in the reverse bridge position with your head and neck supported by the ball. Tighten your abdominal muscles.

2. Start with the weights held just above your shoulders.

3. Slowly raise your arms, keeping your shoulder blades in contact with the ball.

4. Hold for a count of five, then return to the starting position.

5. Do single-arm raises for an extra challenge to pelvic and spinal stability.

2

COOL DOWN

LEG LIFT AND CROSS

Just as important as warming up before exercising is cooling down afterwards. Help your body return to normal in a gentle way by taking time to perform cooling-down stretches at the end of an exercise session. As well as helping to prevent dizziness and a sudden drop in body temperature (which can make you feel unwell), cooling down realigns working muscles to their normal position to avoid post-exercise tightness and stiffness. Cooling-down stretches can be held for longer than ten seconds because the muscles are warm.

2

3

1. Lie on your back with your legs out straight and your arms stretched out to the sides.

2. Breathe in to prepare, and tighten your abdominal muscles. Lift your right leg up towards the ceiling as you breathe out, and flex your foot.

3. Using your abdominal muscles to control the movement, lower your leg across your body, over to the left side, until the foot touches the floor.

4. Hold for a count of 20, then slowly return to the starting position. Repeat on the other side.

TIP

If you can't take your foot all the way to the floor, bend your arm up to meet your foot and rest the foot on your hand.

SEATED SPINAL TWIST

This movement stretches and rotates your abdomen, ribs and spine and stretches your hip muscles. Make sure you move from your hips up, not from your shoulders down.

1. Sit up straight with your legs out in front of you.

2. Bend your right knee and pull your right foot in to your left buttock. Bend your left knee and place your left foot on your right knee.

1

TIP
Aim to keep your spine straight throughout and don't arch your back.

3. Gently draw your navel in towards your spine to set your abdominal muscles and slowly rotate to the left. Use your left hand to help keep your body upright. Rotate as far as is comfortable and hold the stretch for at least a count of 15.

4. Release and return to the start position, then rearrange your legs so that your right leg is on top and rotate to the other side of your body.

3

HIP AND THIGH STRETCH

Be sure to pull in your abdominal muscles during the whole of the hip and thigh stretch in order to protect your back.

1. Kneel with one knee above the ankle and the foot flat on the floor, and stretch your other leg behind you so that the knee touches the floor.

2. Place your hands on your front knee to balance yourself. Hold this position for a count of ten, then repeat on the other leg.

CAUTION
Use a padded exercise mat to protect your knees from bruising.

2

STANDING FULL BODY STRETCH

1. Stand tall with your arms by your sides and your feet hip-width apart.

2. Raise your arms above your head and clasp your hands together.

3. Stretch your arms up as high as possible and feel the stretch in your arms, chest, stomach, hips and thighs.

4. Hold for a count of ten, then release.

LYING FULL BODY STRETCH

If you have any back problems, keep your knees bent slightly throughout this exercise. Also, be aware that if you are unused to stretching you may feel tightness in your shoulders or cramp in your feet – in which case, relax. You will be able to hold this stretch for longer with practice.

1. Lie flat on your back and relax. Breathe in and extend your arms outwards and backwards so that they meet behind your head. Try to keep your arms on the floor throughout the movement but if this isn't possible just keep them as low as possible.

2. Gently stretch out your body from your fingertips to your toes. Your lower back may lift from the floor a little.

3. Hold for a count of 20, then slowly release, bring your arms back down to your sides and relax.

KNEE HUG

This will stretch and release the muscles in your lower back.

1. Lie on your back with your legs in the air and your knees bent.
Tighten your abdominal muscles to protect your lower back.

2. Lift your knees to your chest and hold on to your shins.

3. Pull your knees in as tightly as is comfortable and hold for at least
15 seconds. Slowly release, return to the start position and repeat.

1

2

3

INDEX